PENNY ARCADE™

ARCADE 8

ONI PRESS

AN ONI PRESS PUBLICATION

PENNY-ARCADE.COM

BY JERRY HOLKINS & MIKE KRAHULIK

Penny Arcade V8: Magical Kids in Danger
This volume collects comic strips from the Penny Arcade website,
originally published online from January 1, 2007 through January 2, 2008.

Edited by George Rohac with Charlie Chu
Published by Oni Press, Inc.

Joe Nozemack publisher
James Lucas Jones editor in chief
Cory Casoni director of marketing
Keith Wood art director
George Rohac operations director
Jill Beaton editor
Charlie Chu editor
Troy Look digital prepress lead

ONI PRESS, INC.
1305 SE Martin Luther King Jr. Blvd.
Suite A
Portland, OR 97214

Become our fan on Facebook: facebook.com/onipress
Follow us on Twitter: @onipress
onipress.com
penny-arcade.com

First edition: August 2012
ISBN 978-1-62010-006-6
Library of Congress Control Number: 2012930685

10 9 8 7 6 5 4 3 2 1
PRINTED IN CHINA

Foreword by Cliff Bleszinski

*I*t doesn't matter how many millions of games you sell, or how many awards you win; for a developer, appearing in a *Penny Arcade* strip and seeing one's comic doppelgänger is how one knows they've truly made it in the video game world.

For 14 years now, Jerry and Mike have, through their comic alter-egos, served as the stewards for a growing kingdom of gamers. Their wry, witty commentary on hot trends, characters, or industry conflicts unlocks the gaming business and lays it bare before millions of readers. They're a digital *Doonesbury* of sorts, providing insight into a fast-paced, unique world. They also stage two amazing festivals each year that bring gamers together, and spearhead a charity that helps unite gamers and harnesses their collective creativity, power, and generosity to help sick children.

Clearly Penny Arcade is a busy organization. But at its core, it is a webcomic that provides regular commentary on video games and the video games industry, which happens to be the industry that I have been a part of for almost 20 years now. (Yeah, *Jazz Jackrabbit* was a long time ago.) In that time I've been part of the team that introduced 16-bit color to mainstream gaming; led the development of *Gears of War*, one of the best-selling console shooters of all time; and helped establish Epic Games as one of the strongest names in the gaming industry. But the first time I appeared in a *Penny Arcade* strip still stands out as a personal career milestone.

It was in 1999 when *Unreal Tournament* had become a big hit for us. One of our pillars at Epic for that game was to make a great shooter, but also to avoid copying the weapon arsenals in other popular shooters. Thus we decided to craft a portable teleporter device instead of simply going with the grappling hook, which had been all the rage in 1998. This decision must have done something for the PA guys, because they featured the device — and me — in their comic that day.

Since then, gaming has grown in popularity and it stands to become even more trendy over the coming years with some outstanding iOS and yes, even Facebook games reaching out beyond the hardcore console crowd to more and more people who otherwise never would have labeled themselves as "gamers."

But when I was growing up in New England, *Penny Arcade* wasn't around yet and loving games as much as I did was not so common. I developed a feeling that there were two types of folks in the world: those who "got" gaming and those who didn't. Deep down I felt wary of those other folks: the outsiders Who Did Not Game. And even as those outsiders creep into our gaming world and the gaming industry behaves more and more like other entertainment industries, focusing on hype and sales over what matters most—the loyal fans. The Penny Arcade Expo shines as a beacon amid the other industry events like E3, which have become hype machines, more Vegas than Burning Man. PAX feels like a pilgrimage for many gamers, a journey to a gaming mecca where they can see upcoming games, rub elbows with the creatives who craft those titles, and just nerd out with other fans about anything gaming related.

I mixed my own pilgrimage to PAX with a homecoming in the spring of 2011 when, with 20 years of my career in games behind me, I returned to New England to attend PAX in Boston. It was a surreal experience to be back in the area where I'd grown up inspired, often alone, by video games, and to be surrounded by a mountain of people who "got" games and who wanted to shake my hand and tell me how much they enjoyed the results of my hard work. My experience and countless others are enabled by Mike and Jerry's own hard work and spirit. It doesn't matter if you play games or make them: if you are a gamer, you will feel welcome at PAX, you will be inspired by Child's Play and you will look forward to their comics and their commentary, some of which fill this very book.

Hats off to you, fellas, and keep up the stellar work.

— *Cliff Bleszinski*
  Design Director at Epic Games
  January 5, 2012
  Cary, NC

Introduction to the Eighth Power

ight books?!?

You've got to understand, I sport a rodent's mental capacity; I have mouse-mind. My whole life is a series of quick, tiny movements, bursts of activity, quickly followed by scheduled bouts of unconsciousness. I don't remember the last *strip*. The only reason I know this is the Eighth Book (?!?) is because Robert put an item on my task list that says:

Introduction, Book 8

and I said *Robert what are you even talking about*.

It's true, though. Ten full years have now been catalogued with the release of this volume, ten years of slow metamorphosis that I hope has resulted in a superior lifeform. Has it? There's a bunch of comics in this book, a hundred at least. Soon, you'll be in a good position to know.

I sometimes wonder how it will be when there are no new *Penny Arcade* comics, when I am writing these books merely to *catch up* with a complete body of work. Even when it's over for every other person here, it won't be over for me. I will shift from active verb to reverent curator. I think I will like that.

— *Tycho Brahe*
Seattle, WA
January 2, 2012

JUST FOR THE ELEBIT

January 1, 2007 Elebits was surprisingly fun! It wasn't the straight-up Wiimote shooting gallery you often get; it was more like a weirdo take on the *Ghostbusters* Proton Pack, a "wriggling energy tentacle" (patent pending) that made multiplayer interactions nuts. You could grab shit with it and then *shake* the aforementioned shit until an entire other kind of shit came out. That's not particularly robust as a description, but hopefully the basic idea is contained.

YOUR HEART IS MY SKY (?)

January 3, 2007 We used to have so many little thingies, didn't we? So many humming doodads, all of which were devoted to a singular purpose. I had a little machine that just played music! I used to have a little machine that just added and subtracted things. You may not believe it, but it's true. I even had a cellphone once that could only make phone calls.

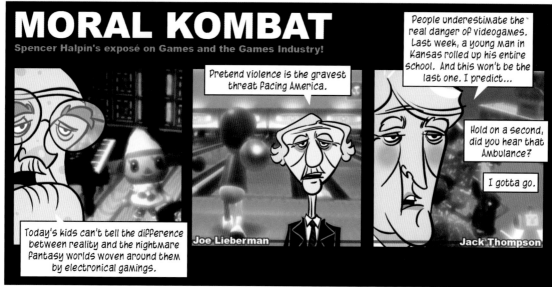

MORAL KOMBAT
Spencer Halpin's exposé on Games and the Games Industry!

People underestimate the real danger of videogames. Last week, a young man in Kansas rolled up his entire school. And this won't be the last one. I predict...

Pretend violence is the gravest threat facing America.

Hold on a second, did you hear that Ambulance?

I gotta go.

Today's kids can't tell the difference between reality and the nightmare fantasy worlds woven around them by electronical gamings.

Joe Lieberman

Jack Thompson

Don't forget: Rainbow Six tonight at ten.

Can't swing it tonight. I'm going to try some Neverwinter with Cheeto.

No, you're not.

I sorta already, you know... planned it.

Yeah, listen... Cheeto. Somebody just called. Your house burned down, and your mom is dead.

Oh my God... MOM! I gotta go!

Be honest with me: are you the devil?

So... R6 at ten?

I SEE WHAT YOU DID THERE

January 5, 2007 It's the same old moral panic whatever-ness that bubbles to the top of our culture from time to time. We could do strips in this vein as often as we wanted, there's certainly enough material for it. The original version of this comic, which never made it past the text file stage, was a much more savage and direct tirade. This kind of obvious political theater legitimately pisses me off. It didn't make for a better comic, though, so we came at it another way.

CHEETO 2: RETURN OF CHEETO

January 8, 2007 Rainbow Six: Vegas — here, reduced simply to the convenient and portable "R6"— was more lifestyle than entertainment product. We even mapped our faces to our characters, which is actually super spooky and weird in practice; watching something that looks *very* much like your friend Kiko be gunned down, bleed, and fall over certainly gives you pause.

THE MICROSOFT ZUNE: 2006-2006

January 10, 2007 Gabriel *now* swears by his Windows Phone, believe it or not, and he enjoys its aesthetic concepts and underpinnings so much that he's legitimately wondering if Windows 8 isn't where he'll switch back. I've tried to explain to him that every other version of Windows is a nightmare realm, and he should reconsider; but their hooks are in 'im with those smooth lowercase text and their "dynamic tiles" or whatever.

OUR SAVAGE FRONTIERS

January 12, 2007 Ah: "Gabriel Is Dumb," one of the many *sub*-genres internal to *Penny Arcade*. A personal favorite, to be sure. This strip is either an independent story OR the preface to a greater work. In that way, "Our Savage Frontiers" is like *Penny Arcade's* version of *The Hobbit*. Gabe and Kara had planned to go to Hawaii years before this, but — as I said in that day's post — Gabriel the Younger did not run his itinerary by *them* when he decided to be born.

THE PILGRIMAGE, PART ONE

January 15, 2007 Robert and I decided that we wanted to finally do the CES thing! See what the vibe was, absorb it to the best of our ability. It seemed more or less foolproof! Theoretically, as staunch technofetishists, it was the sort of environment which could be reasonably assumed to nourish us. Also, it takes place in Las Vegas, which is where they keep all of the Las Vegas.

THE PILGRIMAGE, PART TWO

January 17, 2007 I have problems constantly in the security line, even when I don't have any human organs in my bag. There is just something about my demeanor, some beta wolf aspect I give off that urges them to dominate me. I don't have it as bad as Robert, though. He's on some kind of watch list, we don't know why, and every time he goes through these goddamn things he gets "The Full Meal Deal." It's robust, it's machine assisted, and it takes place in a soundproof room.

THE PILGRIMAGE, PART THREE

January 19, 2007 Oh! So, about CES. I've discussed it before, but unless you were going there to cover the event, I can't imagine how it could hold someone's interest. It might be a huge television, but once you've seen it, it's just another object. Also, there's tons of other televisions there, and once you've seen the biggest one, you sort of wonder what you're gonna do with the rest of your day. I like this stuff, and I like what it enables, but I don't worship it as some elemental force.

THE PILGRIMAGE, PART FOUR

January 22, 2007 He would have enjoyed the whole Consumer Electronics thing substantially more than I did, which is to say that his enjoyment would rate as a positive integer. You can see here that even across thousands of miles (or thousand, singular? I don't actually know, I'm not good at Earth) the event's erotic payload was transferred. The process is entirely mysterious — it's never fully explained how this scenario managed to occur. It would be an incredible case study.

THE HOOK, THE LINE, AND THE SINKER

January 24, 2007 For a super long time, before the "MMO" nomenclature had even been developed, games with a monthly subscription were considered the domain of the ultramega-hardcore. Then *World of Warcraft* obliterated the core of the distinction, and people you'd expect to be completely unfamiliar with this kind of stuff know who Hogger is all the sudden. Paying every month was considered a corrosive force initially; the ire people held toward that practice was transferred to DLC, and then from DLC to the nefarious Online Pass.

THE FEDERAL BUREAU OF TAKING ALL YOUR SHIT

January 26, 2007 In that day's post, I emphasized the distinction between now and then — a threat like this, uttered over Game Chat, resulted in an FBI raid. When I was young, it was simply an accepted fact that some kids were weird. I was weird. I said weird shit people didn't entirely like. When people fucked with me, I'd spin some grisly nonsense about their demise. Generally the response was to leave those people alone, and for the school counselor to nod with a tentative smile. That's not how it works anymore.

IT IS A SENSITIVE TOPIC

January 29, 2007 This is practically a transcription, if not of his *actual words*, than of the hidden language scratched into his onyx heart. From the post: "...he feels as though he is flipping a coin via some elaborate, unaccountable mechanism — a single coin that takes an hour to flip. It is his belief that there are other things he could be doing. For example (and this is just something I came up with off the top of my head) he could be playing a game where his input is correlated with the outcome in some way."

TACT AND DIPLOMACY

January 31, 2007 He really did need an assistant.

THE MANIFOLD FACES OF VISTA

February 2, 2007 The weird thing is that there really was a red AIDS version, although we should probably put the parentheses on there, so that it looks like (RED). There are a number of products affiliated with the project, which is sort of a public/private profit sharing charity engine thingy. We were linked to (RED) laptops with smashing (RED) Windows wallpapers very soon after the strip went up.

IT'S REALLY NOT THAT HARD

February 5, 2007 One of the great pleasures compiling these… compilations, I guess would be the word, is to see how things actually do change. Gabriel reads constantly now, largely due to the advent of the Kindle/Nook/etcetera. He's not indiscriminate, though: he will only read a book if it has a space station, an alien world, or a spaceship on the cover. Preferably all three. I have heard him refer to this unique configuration as "The Holy Trinity."

A RETURN TO TRADITION

February 7, 2007 Yup! There's Div, doing his Div thing. In the same way that politicians once declared "No New Taxes," I have more or less declared "No New Div" when it comes to the writing process. Gabriel resents this, and it is a source of constant tension which sometimes results in frenzied wrasslin'. The reality, though, is that we've done this strip already, with him, in this way. I don't really know what he's for anymore, and until I figure that out, he's on the bench.

THE MOST RECENT CATASTROPHE

February 9, 2007 This is one of my favorite comics. In fact, I think it may be one of my favorite images in general. I love (which is to say, hate) this local news huckster. This was in reference to a nonsensical story about how child molesters were going to Pictochat with your kids while you were both driving on the freeway.

I have a fantasy where we've only got another generation or so of this shit, where the next generation of parents have actually grown up surrounded by technology and don't harbor a primitive fear of it. There are privacy and safety concerns that come with ubiquitous technology, and we'll be better able to manage them if we aren't engaged in a perpetual snipe-hunt.

WE ACCEPT PAYPAL AND MOST MAJOR CREDIT CARDS

February 12, 2007 This many years on, you might not recall just how fraught these console war skirmishes were. Things simply weren't going well for Sony, and every interview was a "savage" slash "rife with barbs."

BIG SAVINGS ON EROTIC ACTS

February 14, 2007 She really isn't a Patriarchy fan, that isn't just something we put in the strip. She's actively opposed to a system of society or government in which men hold the power — a power which women are largely excluded from. She doesn't like the New England Patriarchs, either. Or… maybe it's the New England Patriots. I don't really follow sports. It's one of the two, certainly. She doesn't like them: that's really the main thing.

THE ONYX OBELISK

February 16, 2007 In a post I wrote before our match, I wrote the following: "those who get within range of my backhand should *know this*: I can drive a ball so quickly and with such *intense* lateral spin that it will bore straight up your dickhole and kink your Vas Deferens, sterilizing you instantly." They didn't need a robot to punish us, though: it was brutal. That match was against SOE Seattle, which no longer exists. They worked for years and years (and years) on a cross-platform MMO called *The Agency*, and then simply disappeared.

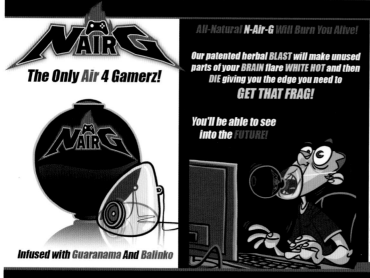

NOW WITH AROMAX

February 19, 2007 It doesn't make me feel "special" when a company thinks that I need my own foods, that there is some nutrient my extreme lifestyle requires. The mystical energy bars pilloried in the strip — which were purported to contain unparalleled levels of "guaranoids and guaranoid compounds" — went out of business a couple years later. I was surprised; these dudes seemed like they were in it for the long haul. They even had a MySpace.

THE HOME OF THE GODS, PART ONE

February 21, 2007 Illusionz was a real arcade, which we loved; that's where we learned to play *DanceDanceRevolution*. It's also where we saw our first Team, which is the DDR equivalent of a Clan. Like so many other examples of the form, Illusionz simply had a hard time evolving to fit a time where processing power is commonplace. OLYMPVS was just a goofy idea, and I'm not sure it would work as an actual business. My guess is that a lot of people have had this fantasy, though, and by doing a strip about it, we could make that fantasy a little more true.

OLYMPUS
Let The Games Begin

By Shep Lovely

It looks like a temple, and maybe it is.

Stepping between the marble columns, I get a nod from the bouncer. I'm in. I return the efficient masculine gesture and enter my "home away from Azeroth," the OLYMPVS. I could have brought the laptop and logged in via the complimentary G, but Olympus is the sort of place one goes to *be there*.

"We don't call it an arcade," remarks Brahe from behind the bar, already making my usual. "But you could certainly call it *Arcadian*."

Like an electronic grove, a copse of lovingly tended arcade classics glow in the perpetual night.

(Right) LEVEL UP The second floor mahogany bar has the libation for your consternation

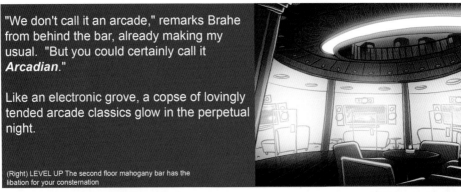

(Left) THE CORE DUO Brahe and Gabriel hold court

(Below) WHAT A RELIEF Welcome back to the stage of history

Wow. This is an incredibly positive article.

Just so you know, I feel *super* bad about burning it down.

THE HOME OF THE GODS, PART TWO

February 23, 2007 I had so much fun trying to write as Shep Lovely; trying to get a grip on that unctuous Complimentary Airplane Magazine tone. Also, pay special attention to the bas relief up in panel one! I suspect Gabriel really enjoyed doing that bit. And apparently you don't pronounce the S in "bas." It's not relief for fish.

LES MOTS DANGEREUX

February 26, 2007 Multiplatform titles were consistently worse, or late, or both, on Sony hardware. The device couldn't even download files in the background, which was… odd. It was farcical to watch this stumbling regent put on such airs, a state of affairs that was only compounded by the gulf between its public pronouncements and reality. They went on like this for years, incrementally improving in price and parity, until I think that now — almost five years hence — we have begun to see the promised eclipse.

YES SOURIS

February 28, 2007 The restaurant had two mice actually, one named Chico, and one named Pico. I don't know if they called Pico that because he was the smaller of the two, or if it was because he had the power of speech and could make his rodent will known. The mouse was like a living coupon, though: if you had the "good fortune" to see him, it turns out they would comp your entire meal. This had the desired effect; I warmed instantly to my tiny benefactor. I raised a glass in his honor, gesturing at the entire dessert menu and suggesting they should "bring me one of all of those."

JOY, AND JOY UNRELENTING

March 2, 2007 Every piece of the "store's" dialogue here represents an actual step in the old purchase process — believe it or not, we didn't add anything. They've made incredible strides since then, to the extent that reading strips from this period is probably strange. There were no trophies back then, don't forget; you couldn't even pull up the XMB during a game. They've come a long way, but they started this generation way, way behind.

IN THE GRIM ETCETERA

March 5, 2007 This was announced all the way back then, and at the time of this writing not much more has been said. Vigil has made other good games, but nothing especially warlike in the grim darkness of the far future. I'll always take an opportunity to talk about *Warhammer 40k* in the strip, though. If you aren't familiar with the setting or don't know why you should be excited, basically, they're making a *Starcraft* MMO. And Blizzard isn't making it, so it will probably come out sometime before you die.

EERIE IN ITS ACCURACY

March 7, 2007 I didn't want to look at some baby pants my wife Brenna had purchased, because I don't care about clothes, and clothes are dumb. That's the actual reason. I would rather look at almost anything else, I would rather look into a magic well and watch my own death. I feel like taking time out to look at clothes says something about you as a person. She told me that not wanting to see these pants meant that I hated our unborn baby. That's not an exaggeration; that is literally what she said.

KARMA SUCKS

March 9, 2007 Ha! Home. We'll have strips about the actual product in another book, but you can see here what a sharp trailer will get you. It was a very good trailer. But they really started to turn our heads with *LittleBigPlanet*, which had all the nods to community and connectivity we were looking for. After watching them flop around and sweat for so long, it was nice to see some good news. I don't actually like to be mean. And I love to be made wrong retroactively.

DARK LESSONS FROM THE DEVIL MACHINE

March 12, 2007 In *Penny Arcade* parlance, the Bench is a visual way of indicating that we're outside the confines of the strip in the same way that the Couch means we are situated within it. It's not an ironclad rule: "Misinformation," seen later in this very book, takes place inside just because it makes more sense. Technically, we made the whole thing up, and it seems like we could do whatever we want, but after thirteen years and counting there's a sense of shared ownership. Occasionally, we feel like stewards of our own creation.

THE OTHER FOOT

March 14, 2007 I am on record as being the only person on Earth who enjoyed *Too Human*. Not when this strip was created, though: the product had not yet materialized, and all anyone had to go on was an old demo that never should have been shown to any living being. Silicon Knights had experienced an especially fraught development cycle on the product, and it was their claim that the Unreal Engine they were using had been misrepresented. This resulted in a lawsuit against Epic, creators of the engine in question, a lawsuit that (at the time of this writing) is still unresolved.

UNFAIR BUSINESS PRACTICES

March 16, 2007 You bet your ass we bought those cookies. I paid and paid until I had no more cash. I paid again when I came back the next day for groceries. I bought them all: waxy, yielding Samoas, fossilized thin mints, anything I could get my hands on. I think I still have them here, somewhere. It was never about actually eating cookies. I wonder if they *give* these girls the crutches, or what. Maybe they should start; it was "super effective," as they say.

GOOD GOD

March 19, 2007 These games are just straight up shocking. It's a combination of many factors, obviously, but an accessible brawler with intriguing depth coupled with the best variation on *Shenmue*'s "Quick Time Event" system to date binds you in its service. QTEs tend to be fairly abstract manifestations of game events — but *God of War* has always tried to hook you into the actions by modeling the motions as closely as possible, like puppetry. For a game where you spend so much time pulling off heads and gouging out eyes, it's surprisingly thoughtful.

EXILE FROM GUYVILLE

March 21, 2007 It was fine! Jesus. It was a perfectly acceptable movie! I just didn't think it was some kind of goddamned manual for living! What am I supposed to do with the information it presents? It's not like I have a convenient cistern around I could kick a mailman into, and getting a gladius would be crazy expensive. I already had every intention of avoiding satyrs. I did get to throw a Liz Phair reference into the title of the strip, though; I guess it wasn't a total wash.

OUR OLD TRICKS

March 23, 2007 We had already obliterated Jack Thompson by this point with a stunt of our own, a substantial donation to charity in his name, which enraged him for some reason. This strip is about the time he filed a countersuit against Take-Two, suggesting that *Penny Arcade* (and others) were involved in racketeering because we all disagreed with him at once. He described us as a kind of attack dog for the industry, which might be true, maybe, if attack dogs were primarily known for biting their masters.

FIRST IMPRESSIONS

March 26, 2007 Tiny games like *Puzzle Quest* end up hard to find sometimes, either as a result of their unparalleled cleverness, an exceptionally short run, or both. *Puzzle Quest* cut right to the heart of it: fluffy pattern matching *stuff* as the engine for an RPG-style number war. So, so cool. It's had many would-be heirs since then who have tried to replicate the formula, including a direct sequel, but for some reason, none of them have ever taken over in the same way, even when they were manifestly more solid as products.

AN EXCERPT FROM THE BOOK OF DEEDS

March 28, 2007 Obviously the specifics of the *Puzzle Quest* experience were somewhat "removed" from the epic events that were supposedly being modeled. It won't surprise you to learn that the systems we engage in games differ from their narrative role, or that the "digested" universe we inhabit in a simulation has been simplified from its inspiration. But it's especially funny in this case, because there's a gigantic rat, low on its haunches, *playing a boardgame*.

Q4 FTW

March 30, 2007 This strip is often referenced online when people discuss this issue, and it's an issue that's being discussed with more frequency. They know precisely how much trouble they are in, and it's only their retail omnipotence that has staved off grim reality. They've responded to this change of epoch in some strange ways: for example, they now have stores that will sell you codes for digital content. I want to make sure everybody's clear: instead of selecting the product from a menu at home, they will sell you a *physical* code you can bring home and type in. THE FUTURE!

PATIENT ZERO

April 2, 2007 Gabriel has a special knack for getting sick before, during, or after a con. His body acts as a natural centrifuge, emerging from or entering these events with the absolute worst, most pure version of whatever pox. This was back when he was still shaking hands at all, before innovations like the Iron Guard Position. I've never been able to fully adapt to not shaking hands; it's a pragmatic solution, certainly, but lacks humanity somehow.

REVOLTING EVEN TO CONTEMPLATE

April 4, 2007 I think it's been over a year now since I've played *Rock Band*, which is genuinely weird to think: I played it every day for years, and now its legacy is a pile of semi-functional plastic buried in yards and yards of knotted cord.

IN THE BEFORE-NOW

April 6, 2007 In my savage and o'ergrown youth, I made choices regarding my body and *some* plants which Gabriel will never forgive me for. Indeed, my life is a gruesome cautionary tale: imagine how many sold out conventions and solvent businesses I'd have without those indiscretions! Also, you should pull up the video for "Jump," by the ATL's Kris Kross. Be aware that you might jump inadvertently. But also, these young men! You can't not love them. They look like they got into dad's closet and went nuts.

A NOVEL TECHNIQUE

April 9, 2007 I did, actually: I had to leave Sakuracon to go back to Spokane for some kind of family thing. Easter or some shit. From that day's post: "This left Gabriel to manage a two-hour panel *by himself* in the convention's largest hall. I was distraught, but only regarding my dereliction and not because I thought he would be unable to manage it. He is the funny one, after all. It has ever been thus: he the damaged genius, and I the loyal archivist who scrambles to collect his mad prophecies."

LAKE FRANZIBALD

April 11, 2007 Franzibald stands in here for David & Goliath owner Todd Goldman, who has come under fire more than once for plagiarizin' them there Internets. Mike Tyndall operates an archive that collects each instance of malfeasance, and it has (rough estimate) ten billion examples. This particular instance was the infamous Dave Kelly/Purple Pussy ripoff, the profits of which Goldman was ultimately made to disgorge. I love that word, disgorge; I celebrate every opportunity to use it.

MATERIAL COMPONENTS

April 13, 2007 In this day's post, the term "motion sensing wand controls" is followed by three separate exclamation points. That should communicate the excitement I felt, excitement which might have been much better served by Wii Motion Plus, which didn't come out for another couple years. This strip is also one of the incredibly rare six panel comics we've done. There are perhaps four of them, total. Maybe five. Actually, I don't remember how many there are. Not many.

AN EXCITING OPPORTUNITY

April 16, 2007 The name isn't authentic, but it's not an unfair characterization of the product we were offered. This is simply a "genre" of application I don't get much use out of. It doesn't work for some reason, I'm not sure why. I don't think that makes me better than other people or anything, it's simply true. There's probably a study out there that explains precisely *why* a simulated, ghoulish, perpetually willing sexoid isn't a super tantalizing proposition. Although, come to think of it, the sentence which precedes this one will probably do in a pinch.

DELUSIONS OF GONDOR

April 18, 2007 *Lord of the Rings Online* toyed around with some of the MMO archetypes a bit to maintain the texture of its revered fiction: you managed systems like "morale" and "dread" to maintain your effectiveness, which was the sort of thing minstrels could help you do. I had a lot of fun in this game, actually: I liked its chapter based progression, and I especially liked how you could write and play music in the gameworld. Plus, I mean… at the time? With everything cranked up? Incredible. Screenshots looked like photographs.

A DUBIOUS METHODOLOGY

April 20, 2007 *Doki Doki Majo Shinpan!* was/is a game about touchin' on tons and tons of witches. Well, potential witches. You don't know if they are or not until you start touching them like crazy! You might think that you could probably do all the touches in one game, that one game could contain them all, but you would be wrong. The game has not one, but *two* sequels. I understand that they offer "an enhanced witch check touching system," which seems good? I guess…?

VICTORY

April 23, 2007 Things were much different earlier in our Game Industry Ping Pong League career. We had, like, seven people, and we'd be playing against places that had a hundred and forty employees. We didn't really have a place to practice, either — the ping pong table *used* to sit diagonally in a room that wasn't big enough for it. There were also some tiles and stuff we couldn't get up, so injuries were common.

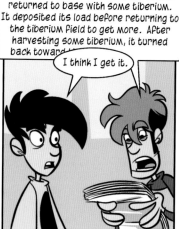

SPHERE FACTOR

April 25, 2007 *Odin Sphere* really is something special, and I almost didn't see it — Atlus often sends us very, very weird things, and I don't always have a chance to absorb them fully. We popped it into the PS2 on a whim, mostly because there was nothing else really going on in the gaming universe. What happened after that is a blur. I woke up several hours later, the controller in my hand, as though I had fallen into a black sleep filled with dark dreams.

DYNAMISM

April 27, 2007 It's actually quite possible to write this sort of tie-in stuff such that it does add something — does improve it. I have to say that reading the first *Dragon Age* book ("The Stolen Throne," I think) before playing the game improved the experience immeasurably. I don't know if I'd have enjoyed DA as much as I did without the benefit of that groundwork. I'd love to write something like this myself, someday. In another universe, perhaps, where time is not such a finite quantity.

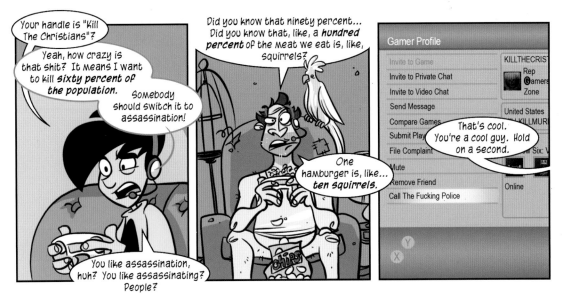

UNIQUE FAUNA

April 30, 2007 Would you believe that the bit in the toxic green speech bubble is an actual quote? We don't know if he actually had a cockatoo, but I don't think its an unreasonable assertion. I made the mistake of spending some time in general chat a couple weeks ago after a multi-year hiatus, and to say that "it has not improved in the interim" doesn't quite capture it. The Party system hadn't been introduced yet, so it could not rescue us. It wasn't integrated until the year after this strip was posted.

THE LIDLESS EYE

May 2, 2007 From that day's post: "*Eye of Judgment* — Sony's unbearably compelling CCG, played with the upcoming Playstation Eye peripheral — may be the most niche product ever conceived. A constructible deck card game that requires a custom camera and a six hundred dollar gaming console to interpret it, 'niche' may be insufficient to describe the tight, sunless, deep sea crevice such a product might reside in. Not that it matters to me, of course: I am the pale white lobster that makes such cracks his home."

THE BROODAX IMPERIATE

May 4, 2007 Ultimately, as more and more of his cells submitted to the incursions of my Boardgaming Ray. Sorry, but I have to quote the post again, because it perfectly captures Old Gabe: "As detailed – um, loosely detailed – in the strip, every molecule of this game would need to be altered in order for Gabriel to like it. In the Gabriel version, players would move bits of red licorice around a sizzling porterhouse, waiting for *their* chance to trade caramel for boobs. The game (at least, as traditionally constructed) is not played on meat."

THE BROODAX ETCETERA

May 7, 2007 One of the things that distinguishes a typical *Penny Arcade* strip, in addition to the radical, in-your-face bestiality, is that we usually try to have our punchline in Panel Two and then leave the "camera" running in panel three to see the aftermath. That's what happened here, because there was no room in the other strip: the situation is, I'm sure you'll agree, fairly weird. And we wanted to show this weirdness for *entirely too long*.

WHAT TO DO IF YOU HAVE PURCHASED SPIDER-MAN 3

A Practical Guide

PAGS Penny Arcade Game Safety

Don't panic.

Simply lie down, and wait to die.

1.

2.

ELITE

- May eat at the Elite table in the lunchroom

- May kick sand on Free Players while at the beach

- Elite players may devour Free Play users at any time

- Elite players may ride Free Play users like mounts

FREE PLAY

- Free Play users may not look upon Elite Players

- Free Play users may not speak to Elite players, even if the Elite player tries to trick the Free Player into speaking to them by saying "What's Up" or "Free Play User Says What"

HELLGATE
LONDON

THE DANGERS OF EXPOSURE

May 9, 2007 Thanks to strips like this one, I'm starting to remember just how rough the transition was to the current generation of consoles. No one ever asked that much of the Wii, it wasn't designed to cash those kinds of checks — but games on the Xbox or the PS2 that had sequels come out on the new systems often had real concerns. Performance was the case here. But there were weird examples too, like *Tiger Woods*, whose next-gen offering had a fraction of the maps.

DISPARITIES

May 11, 2007 *Hellgate: London* was kind of a crazy ride, huh? It's just been *re*-released as an F2P at the time of this writing, years after it (and the company that created it) collapsed. It had other problems, certainly, but I often wonder if that won't be a better model for the game. It wasn't all a wash, though: a exploratory project running off-site, in a tiny corner of the company, eventually metastasized, or... benevolized, maybe, and became *Torchlight*. So maybe everything turned out okay.

THE THIRD TIME

May 14, 2007 It is the official editorial position of our site that the campaigns in a *Halo* game generally aren't the best, and that the multiplayer is real, real good. Where things get inverted is with *Halo: ODST*, which is supposedly the worst one by general appraisal, when it is actually the finest campaign in the entire series. It gets there by being well written, having a novel structure, and by featuring *actual human beings as characters*.

JIM BEAM

May 16, 2007 See, back then, we didn't even know about the Spartan Laser! That's why we had to call it out. It wasn't real until someone invented it, which is always the strange thing to realize as you travel back in time with a compilation like this. Now it's of a piece with the nailguns from *Quake* or whatever — legend. It used to be my job on this map to run up to the laser and guard Kiko while he got it, and I did so. I'm very good at absorbing bullets.

THE SUGGESTION BOX

May 18, 2007 Before the ill-fated *Lair*, Factor 5 was largely known to us via their *Star Wars* offerings: action-oriented shooters crafted with painstaking attention to the setting. For opinions on the dragon-based shooter, try a slice from that day's post: "My limited playtime with the game has only encouraged me to *further limit* said playtime, throttling this value until it reaches zero." Of course, this was considered heresy, but only by people who had never played it.

THE RISING COST OF ROCK

May 21, 2007 This was back when people were buying music games at all, I suppose. Moving on: I have written two songs under the Sex Generals moniker, "Are You Really A Woman" and "Warmachine," the second one being for charity. The Sex Generals are mostly me and John Drake from Harmonix. We try our best to make music that is Good Bad, that is to say, music that's Bad On Purpose. That's as opposed to Bad Bad, which is just regular old "bad."

ON THE KEEPING OF SECRETS

May 23, 2007 This kind of message control is pretty incredible, you have to admit. I mean, I have sources in any western company you could care to name. I know every goddamn thing. I have sources in Blizzard, too, but they never tell me anything until it gets announced for real. On the day such an announcement might take place, I will receive a mail from one of them immediately afterward with a single smiley-face emoticon. And that's it.

NOW, WE MAY SPEAK

May 25, 2007 We ended up with an invitation to some kind of press thing here in town, "town" in this case meaning "Seattle," and since it was fifteen minutes away and we love to raid catering trays, we hopped on board. This was in the cool middle of Nintendo's mainstream opus, and most of what was there didn't have much gravity for us. *Super Mario Super Strikers Ultra Charjitos* (or whatever) got a grip on us though. We loved the first one, and *Soccer Slam* before it; I guess we like Soccer when you take out most of the "soccer."

THE COMING APOKÉLYPSE

May 28, 2007 It is genuinely strange that we were able to resist this game's primal sorcery for so long, but once it managed to take hold, its toxic quills got in deep. Once he'd wrapped up the campaign proper, infected his creatures with the Pokérus, and completed an EV training regimen, we started taking this rough crew of his online to no little success. I adopted my classic role, which is to act as a combination cheerleader/vizier/human Pokédex.

Congratulations, you have completed Dirty Dancing: The Game.

Aw, man...

Now: *Open your front door.*

We can cut all this down later. Go ahead, anytime you're ready.

Well, we're The Moderators, and we think that epic tales are being told every day on gaming message boards.

So... You act out forum threads. Do you think that's accurate?

What we do is challenge the audience.

These are powerful stories. Hidden stories. And they're written in the language of our time.

Fact: Lair is awesome and lok as if real life movie.

Sign - It have mountains, oceans, and desserts. Cel proceling.

Meh

THE TIME OF HIS LIFE

May 30, 2007 The Swayzophilia on display here is at the very threshold of my tolerance, but *Penny Arcade* is a partnership and I must yield on occasion to balance the Karmic Wheel. Anyway, this is how games *should* end. That's how it can feel, sometimes, but this is how it should be: all of your friends are there, they're clapping, there are *snacks*, and an immortal Patrick Swayze hoists you to a place of honor and complete freedom.

OUR RICH CULTURE

June 1, 2007 We have a real enthusiasm for message boards: their unique grammar, their moist ecology, and actually, let's say their grammar again because it really can be incredibly strange. Often in cases like these, we turn to Mr. Period and The Bad Boys Of Punctuation to shed light, but for some reason we decided to go high concept on this one with a theatre troupe. To get a sense of what we were going for, look up a review called "Dot Dot Dot." It's worth it.

THE CHANGING WORKFORCE

June 4, 2007 I still think *Shadowrun* in its updated form — a class-based shooter in the vein of *Tribes* — was incredibly fun. As the standard-bearer for some competitive, cross-platform fantasy maybe it didn't succeed, probably because people don't actually want that kind of shit, but as a game that you *play* and *is fun* it didn't have much to answer for. Its Glider is one of the more satisfying traversal methods yet. Also: The belt up there, hanging from the horn? A very, very nice touch. One point to Gabriel.

RETREAT TO THE CITADEL

June 6, 2007 I never had a chance to play it, not the *Halo* version at least, but generally, you can get a lot of fun out of that system. Most people I know focused on the mainstream/indie comics figs, but I was inexorably drawn to the *Mechwarrior* version. Having been a *Battletech* player in my youth, it was nice to have an echo of that. It was by no means as crunchy as its forebear, but it did have a tasty sort of snacky thing going on. If *Battletech* was a Cool Ranch Dorito, *Mechwarrior* had a kind of Pop Chips thing going on.

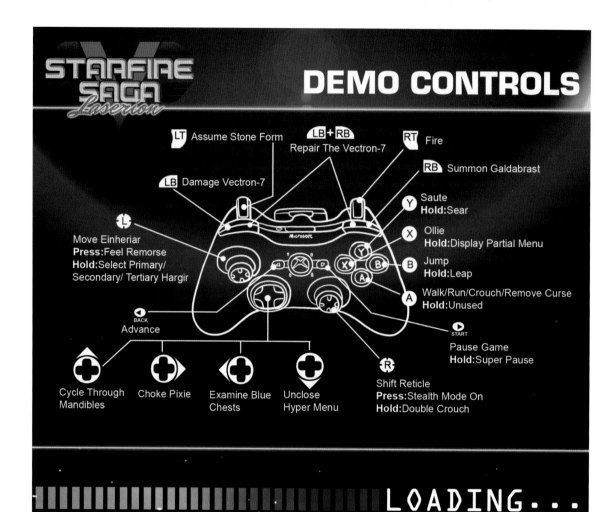

FROM THE MAKERS OF "BEAM KINGS"

June 8, 2007 This is one of my favorite comics of ALL TIME. I have a hunger for jokes in diagrams, it's something about the juxtaposition of explicit labeling with discrete items that are conceptually vague. Maybe. But you can fit so many strange ideas into a construction like this: What is a Galdebrast, for example? Is it good to summon one? How about a Hargir? Why is it necessary to have so many? These are the questions that burn at its very heart.

MY LATEST ASSAULT

June 11, 2007 This used to happen a lot, and it eventually built up to the point where I flipped out. We talk about Solitaire and *Pac-Man* in the strip, but what really sent me over the edge was a review of Xevious. First of all, you don't talk shit about fucking *Xevious*. Second of all, the game was getting scored a four out of ten for graphics and a four out of ten for sound. As opposed to what motherfucker, Crysis?! What are we even comparing this shit to? GRAAAA!

GABRIEL ASCENDANT

June 13, 2007 The demo is probably up, still: it was essentially a racer with some trick stuff built in, pretty normal fare, but when we played it six years ago or whatever it wasn't without its charms. We have kids now, and thus are much more likely to be exposed to software designed for children. Some of this stuff is pretty nasty. Young people don't have a base of experiences to compare things to, so they get a lot of reheated clones. Not always, but often. Sometimes they're surprisingly great, so great that you wonder how it could possibly have happened.

SEARCH BLOG

A blog by SCEA for Playstation® fans.

Welcome to
Playstation.Blog

SUBSCRIBE TO THE PLAYSTATION BLOG

CATEGORIES
- Developer Corner
- Find Us
- Hardware
- Industry Outlook
- Playstation Network
- Statements
- Title Spotlight

Jun 15 — In Memoriam
+ Posted by Jack Tretton // President & CEO

John Travolta
2003-2007

[Mood / ☻ Reflective]
[Song / Elton John - Candle in The Wind]

PLAYSTATION CONVERSATION

A collection of PlayStation news and links from around the web.

Playstation 3 Saves Baby Girl From Wolf - Joystiq
+ Posted 06 14 07 04 12 PM

Playstation 3 Actually Super Affordable - 1up
+ Posted 06 14 07 03 26 PM

New PSP: Two Screens, Stylus Controls - PSP Fanboy
+ Posted 06 14 07 03 18 PM

Developers To Sony: "You Are So Great!" - GameBizDaily
+ Posted 06 13 07 04 14 PM

Blu-Ray Voted "Best Ray of 2007" - RayWatch
+ Posted 06 13 07 03 33 PM

Jun 15 — I walk a lonely road
+ Posted by Jack Tretton // President & CEO

Ugh. No posts today.

[Mood / ☻ Hopeless]
[Song / Green Day - Boulevard Of Broken Dreams]

READER COMMENTS

In Memoriam
I didn't know your cat but i had a cat once and i am sad about your cat...
+ InvaderTim

I walk a lonely road
I m sending out positive nrg... Hope u r receeving!!...
+ Panah

I walk a lonely road
Never stop posting - John Travolta would want you to keep...
+ Deadly Peach

...
omg that = sux
+ golgothain

What Will They Think Of Next?!?!
I like fried chicken but i've never had fried other things, maybe it's good?...
+ Sawblaide

Jun 14 — ...
+ Posted by Jack Tretton // President & CEO

John Travolta got hit by a car today. Not the real John Travolta, my cat John Travolta. I was totally bumming over analysts' predictions of Sony's profitablity for fiscal year 2007-2008 a couple weeks ago, but JT curled up in my lap and fixed me up. She was an awesome cat and she will live on through the lives she touched.

[Mood / ☻ Shocked]
[Song / The Fray - How To Save A Life]

Jun 13 — What Will They Think Of Next?!?!
+ Posted by Jack Tretton // President & CEO

<T-Rex> did you know that te guy who invented fried snickers is frying coke now?
<kazmania776> !!!
<T-Rex> he like puts the coke in some dough and fries it.
<T-Rex> the whole thing is totally crazy
<T-Rex> he is like a frying pioneer
<kazmania776> no no! he's like a fryoneer
<T-Rex> LOL
<T-Rex> this is totally getting posted

[Mood / ☻ Hungry!]
[Song/ Gym Class Heroes - Cupid's Chokehold]

QUICK POLL

How awesome is the Playstation 3?

● So Awesome

VOTE   View Results

ARCHIVES
+ June 2007

REQUIESCAT IN PACE

June 15, 2007 Sony finally deigned to "blog" this year, inaugurating it with a blog from CEO Jack Tretton, which I described as "like having Poseidon clean your pool."

TYCHO BRAHE, OFFICE PARIAH

June 18, 2007 I played *Pokémon* long enough to understand it, and then the lid closed forever — annihilating all the tiny lives entrusted to my care. I was the only one who managed to escape though, as you see. This happens often. My role is to scout out the *next* game, so after my friends have set up a base camp in a particular title or genre my compulsion is to seek new pastures. It's a role I often share with Kiko, assuming he doesn't get hooked too deep by one of our discoveries.

THAT TERRIBLE GRIP

June 20, 2007 This one was alright, but the one for *Halo 2* — "I Love Bees" — was an experience I preferred over the game it was trying to promote! "ILB" was an entirely new shape for a story, a science fiction tale where the telling *itself* was a kind of science fiction. Hundreds of people, across an entire country, playing psychiatrist to a wounded artificial intelligence? Good lord. More of this, please.

PERFECTLY REASONABLE

June 22, 2007 From that day's post:

"Gabriel and Kara are thinking about moving, but only *one* of them is approaching things with the correct amount of dread. It is almost impossible to find a home these days which is *not* some unholy conduit — a winking anus of evil that acts as a revolving door for hell's starveling dead. But a hollowed-out ghoul in shredded wedding gown doesn't need to be a dealbreaker. Don't let a sundered soul turn *your* dream home into a nightmare charnel house!

Basic Research Is Critical. For example: if you're moving into what was once an old farmstead, it's even odds that a failed fertility ritual resulted in darkness unending for an unsuspecting bride. Where do you think those prize pumpkins *come* from? Here's a hint: It ain't Miracle-Gro.

Make Yourself A Vessel For Unlife. Probably don't need to explain that one; it's pretty straightforward. Sixth son of a priest, bound in silver chains, etc.

After that, you simply **Perform The Forbidden Ritual**. Prick your ring finger with mistletoe, and with the help of a necromancer wed the lonely spectre in blasphemous reverse marriage ceremony. It's best to perform this one during the Winter Solstice, when our realm and the next brush against one another."

A COGENT ARGUMENT AGAINST FAITH

June 25, 2007 From that day's post:

"The goddamned Dorito people are now exhorting gamers to create game ideas based on chips, which I took as a powerful theological argument. They suggest that gamers may find inspiration in their "iconic shape," by which I assume they mean "a triangle." These "Chip Lords" can't even be bothered to make their own commercials anymore. They have heard about the YouTube MySpaces, and they want to get an oily tendril around participation culture.

Somehow we ended up with a bag of their X-13D superchips, some kind of mystery flavor, and if you want to know what they *taste* like imagine that a hamburger patty has fallen onto a cat, condiment side *down*. Believe me, it's worth buying a bag to verify this assertion. I went to their site to try and figure out what was going on, or if I should call Poison Control, or what, and it took me to some terrifying snack chip dystopia. I ended up working these weird gears and twisting valves so cheese could get through, it was like the nacho version of *Myst*."

SUPERB TECHNIQUE

June 27, 2007 On their website, they included the following disclaimer: "Based in the UK, Three Speech isn't part of PlayStation, but it does get to speak to PlayStation. You could say we're 'semi official'." I guess I don't know how to parse that entirely. That seems like some goddamned nonsense to me, but I have (at times) been called a cynic. Maybe it was totally cool, on the up and up, etc. But, wow. That doesn't really express the rich, raw extent of your editorial freedom.

THE FACTS OF THE MATTER

June 29, 2007 We borrowed Brent from our friend Scott Kurtz here, playing around with the storyline he was running at the time. I probably use my iPhone for one thing or another every seven and a half minutes or so, so it's hard to imagine a time when I didn't have it — but I didn't, because nobody had it then. They weren't real yet. The iPhone we picked up the day after this strip was posted didn't even have iTunes, or an App Store. There were no "apps." And it was *still* amazing.

THE LINE EXPERIENCE

July 2, 2007 I remember this day quite well. It was super weird: when you finally got in to buy your phone, all the employees would applaud you as though you had just done something momentous. In retrospect, I guess that wasn't entirely wrong. Also, the guy "behind" Gabriel there is Wil Shipley, who you may recognize from other strips. There were a few years there where he made it a point to win the "Appearance In A Strip" auction at the Child's Play dinner.

ALTERNATE VERSION: We did a second version of the strip and dropped it in the post, to pay tribute to Wil Shipley's famous demeanor. He has a reputation in the Apple Development community for being... well, for being himself. He is the one who first talked to Gabriel about medication for OCD, so we owe him a great debt. He did offer us an edit to the strip: he says that in his circle, giving Steve Jobs the handjob would have been the real honor. We took his word on it.

THE REIMAGINING

July 4, 2007 I have described the memories of those who came of age in the eighties as "a kind of ghastly rummage sale," a mausoleum to be raided on the cheap. But there are hard limits on what can actually survive these grim resuscitations, or at least, I hope there are. I could be wrong on this one: the next strip is pretty awesome.

EXCERPTS FROM "RUXPIN"

July 6, 2007 There is literally NOTHING about this comic that isn't a) dope, b) fly, or c) fresh for realz. Every panel deals piercing damage. In this case, the thing being pierced is your resolve. You want to be angry, angry at how ridiculous this entire exercise is, but your human skin is tingling. You find yourself inexorably drawn to the exquisitely formed bear in Panel 2, regardless of gender. You know, somewhere deep down, that *every square inch of him is warm*.

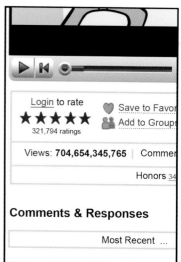

A PRIVET MATTER, PART ONE

July 9, 2007 I'm trying to figure out the right time to introduce *Harry Potter* books to my young son. I read them when I was an adult, because that's when they came out — the first three books were a wedding present, actually. But if you go back through and read them, they're scary as shit! That school is not in any way safe. It's chockablock with sorcerous phylacteries, murderous flora, and high-level monsters with instakill attacks. It's a marvel any of these goddamned kids got out of there alive.

A PRIVET MATTER, PART TWO

July 11, 2007 You never know when we're going to decide that something is worthy of a follow-up. Right? Looking at that first strip, I might not be all like "let's crank up the sequel machine," except that when I *was* in a position to do so, I did exactly that! Yeah, okay; snakes, it's some kind of jungle thing, whatev. For someone who claims to revile "dreaded continuity," I apparently can't get enough. I'm always flicking the crook of my elbow, trying to coax up a vein.

THE NEW WORLD

July 13, 2007 The *Galaxies* he was talking about were, specifically, *Galaxies* of the *Super Mario* variety. I love this game; I can't really say enough good about it. Nintendo's trick, and it's a good one, is their capacity to give you something you already liked once again, and let you have it for the first time. *Galaxies* was a great game, and it was unmistakably a Mario game, but the addition of the pointing gameplay (which revealed especially satisfying "stretching" interactions) feels inexplicably situated in the series' ancient lexicon.

BRAINS WITH URGENT APPOINTMENTS

July 16, 2007 I'm getting better at simply *absorbing* entertainment, which is to say I'm getting worse at fighting the pop cultural behemoth. There's an amazing quote from the play slash movie, *Hurlyburly*, to the effect of "Good taste has no doubt deprived me of a great many things." That used to be my response when Gabriel wanted me to watch movies like *Face/Off* or some freeze-dried reconstitution of *G. I. Joe*. Now I just fill my mouth with Mike and Ikes, and let the films wash over me.

SHUCKING: A TUTORIAL

July 18, 2007 The demo in question had already been released in Europe, but for some reason the US version had been attached to this booklet thing. Was this the last time such a thing had happened? Where I went to purchase a *Magazine* that included a *Disc* that included a couple hundred megs of data on it? And then it didn't work, so I had to boil the disc in a pot to make it readable again? These rituals! No-one born today will ever believe this was something we actually did.

A FABULOUS INVENTION

July 20, 2007 *Chore Wars* (as you might recall) is one of them there "gamification" engines which is designed to add the now standard progression mechanics to regular shit you might do with your *linens*. I use something a little broader conceptually for a to-do list called *EpicWin*, which is marvelous. The office also experimented with *Fitocracy* for a bit, an exercise tracker, which we ended up doing a strip about in 2011. That's a spoiler, I guess…? Avert your eyes!

THE TOURNÉMON, PART ONE

July 23, 2007 Also a fact: my associate Gabriel attended tournaments fairly regularly during this time. *Pokémon Diamond* was his first real experience with the franchise beyond half-hearted dabbling, and it had him bad. I could say that it had him *like* something, like some kind of a *Pokémon* for example — one that could really get hold of a person. Maybe with some big claws, or an implacable seizing mandible. I'm sure there's one like that. I only know about *Pokémon* while I have the strategy guide open.

THE TOURNÉMON, PART TWO

July 25, 2007 This is a true Pork Fact, by the way; if you ask him about it, he will say yes. This isn't something he considers strange in any way. This is a wholly normal lifestyle choice. All the stuff you're supposed to do organically, all the special trades and whatnot, assume something like a schoolyard environment where Pokémania is an assumption. He's merely simulating that scenario at home, *under rigorous mathematically optimal laboratory controls.*

THE TOURNÉMON, PART THREE

July 27, 2007 I'm kind of obsessed with sign language. Well, I'm obsessed with language in general, but being able to communicate with real specificity in the absence of a verbal component is incredibly useful.

We taught my son to sign before he was capable of the *mouth words*, and it was fucking incredible to watch him invent his own signs and to create compound signs completely without input from us. A blackberry briar somehow became a "hurt-tree," a helicopter was a "fan-airplane," that kind of shit. We're built to communicate; that's not especially shocking as far as statements go. It's another thing altogether to watch a goddamn infant iterate the simple rules you've given them and embroider a custom lexicon.

THE TOURNÉMON, PART FOUR

July 30, 2007 Wow. So… that went to a dark place, huh? To paraphrase Anton Chekhov, "If there's a pedophile on the mantle in Act One…"

In order to play Eye of Judgment, you will need:

Playstation 3

Eye Of Judgment Software

Playstation Eye Peripheral

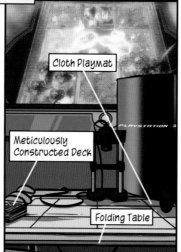

Cloth Playmat

Meticulously Constructed Deck

Folding Table

Someone Else Who Is As Crazy As You Are

Wait a second... So you're saying *men* can be librarians?

Yes. That's what I'm saying.

Well, what do they call them?

Librarians.

I thought *librarian* implied gender, like... like "sorceress."

I don't know. It just seems like they should have another name.

I like *Libratorr.*

No, I've got it. *Librarymans!*

JUDGMENTAL

August 1, 2007 I was obsessed with this game, I think it's fair to say. A smart, compact, combination tactics and collectible cards, it was systemic genius. It was incredibly hard to find cards for it up here, and by the time my back-ordered cards arrived, people were putting together brutally efficient decks using cards they'd printed out from the Internet. There were problems! I'd never say there weren't. It just meant playing with friends by appointment, which was probably the best way to play it anyhow.

THE COUCH DIALOGUES

August 3, 2007 Another word-for-word rendering of an actual conversation. We were talking to the dudes from *Unshelved*, which is a comic about the things mothafuckas be getting up to in the library. Words are funny things, though. My wife, who has a degree in theatre and everything, says that internal to the craft the word "actress" doesn't even exist; there are only actors. I'd never heard that before. Come to think of it, I've never heard it since, either. So who knows.

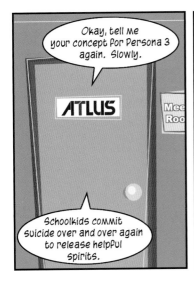

POTENT YET TROUBLING IMAGERY

August 6, 2007 That's really what you do! You really shoot your OWN MAGICAL HEAD. Well, sort of. The imagery is all there, and the emotional reality is there, but it's the tiniest bit more complex. We imagined that this would be a point of contention with Those People Who Are Always Angry About Something In A Videogame They'll Never Play Because They Don't Actually Play Videogames, And The Medium Only Exists When There's An Opportunity For Hand-Wringing Or Tsk-Tsking.

I KNOW A GUY

August 8, 2007 I don't know how this story shakes out medically, if gums even have that kind of voltage, or like if they're AC or DC or what. But this is a story which was told to me in confidence by a "guy I know." That is to say, I *know* him. And, as I'm sure you are aware, things which are told to you via an unnamed third party are almost certainly true. And now *I'm* telling you this thing, which *seems* like it would make the whole thing even more tenuous when what it actually does is transmute it into pure fact!

OUR HELPFUL GUIDE

August 10, 2007 This used to be a thing, all this stuff! A franchise war between brands in a part of the industry that hardly exists anymore took up feet upon feet of screen space. I played *Rock Band* most days for probably two years. Short of a Massively Multiplayer game, I've never had that kind of dedication to any game.

SOFT TARGETS

August 13, 2007 The game this strip is referring to — John Woo's *Stranglehold* — is one where you slide around on shit and shoot a mothafucka in *the slowest of motions*. I played the tiny part they give you in the demo for hours and hours. It's got that *Max Payne* vibe where you can "choreograph" great looking sequences that are also successful as gameplay, and I generally like that kind of "performance" aspect. We were just goofing around here, but they added this Achievement in the DLC.

OUR CONTINUING SERIES

August 15, 2007 There was a time when *BioShock* was new. New! You didn't *know* yet if you were entitled to sweat off your brow, or what different aspects of our SO CALLED DEMOCRACY felt entitled to this sweat. You had not yet fired angry bees from your hand, which had been transformed into a living hive. The thing to do if you want to prove that you're an innovative free thinker is to say bad things about *BioShock*, and it's possible to, certainly. But in aggregate, there were so many incredible ideas in that world.

A DARK RECIPE

August 17, 2007 There was a magical period, as there sometimes is before an official release date, where a few copies slorp through the gate and run into the wild. I was not able to secure one; but I never fail to *attempt*. Getting something early is its own reward; there was that year when 7-Eleven was selling games for some reason, do you remember that? They didn't give a shit about dates. You could buy any game they had, even if there was a napalm orange sticker on the top which said "DO NOT SELL."

DELIGHT YOUR FRIENDS WITH THESE FUN FACTS

August 20, 2007 It was during this time that someone made a way to cross-reference Wikipedia edits with specific IPs, which meant that you could see precisely what self-serving edits people and corporations were making. I only edited Wikipedia a single time, and it was after this debacle, so I didn't get scooped up in it. I edited a page to say that a famous person, I don't remember exactly who, was actually a lobster.

MY COMEUPPANCE

August 22, 2007 I have to say, I like the idea that everything you do in this game can fall under the single heading "art." People really seemed to like this comic, and by "people" I mean designers, clamoring instantly for garments featuring this imaginary product. There are a couple games that are sort of like Photoshop Hero; but then they came out with *Scribblenauts* and *Super Scribblenauts*, and I began to pulse with power.

HARROWING, SAYS GAMESPOT

August 24, 2007 I liked this thing! I must have, to try and work it into so many strips. I was happy when the Move came out because it meant I could use my camera. Of course, I can only really have one videogame camera situated in the correct place at a time, which means that sometimes it's hanging off the back of the "entertainment center" (read: shelf) from its thick cord. It's like the "bench" I guess. Right? I mean, it's not off the team.

ON PAX (AND ALSO PACKS)

August 27, 2007 This was the strip drawn at that year's PAX, which was the first time Gabriel ever approached the tabletop room for his own purposes instead of at my grave insistence or because I had physically dragged him to the location. That has become one of my favorite parts of the show, easily, and I suspect I'm not alone. The second PAX East had the biggest room for it yet, with multiple stores on the floor itself and so many people you had to go to a skywalk above to see them all.

ALTERNATE VERSION: If you have never attended the Create A Strip panel, you might not know that Gabriel takes "requests" while he's drawing them. These requests sometimes make it into the strip proper, but sometimes they're saved on a separate layer, like so.

TO CATCH A PREDATOR: RAPTURE

August 29, 2007 Very weird, all that Little Sister stuff. Weirder still when, through the normal course of playing the game, you find their little indoctrination center and absorb the freaky propaganda they fill them up with. Oh, and also, their bodies have been rejiggered to drink and store genetic material. And they're protected by conscious diving bells full of angry guts. I'm starting to think "weird" might be insufficient.

PENDULOUS AND VILE

August 31, 2007 See?!? This is the kind of thing you would use your camera for! It usually took a long time, and then when it was finally complete there was always something goofy about it. For example, a foul and/or greasy pallor that you can never quite remove. Even if you did get it damn near perfect, now it was just… bizarre somehow, especially in comparison to the standard models. The novelty factor was incredibly high, and it did allow for feline golfers, but usually we'd revert to the standard tools.

WHAT PEOPLE ARE SAYING

September 3, 2007 Holy shit. If you want to see me chew, I mean *really* chew on a game, check the post for this one. A sample: "There are some who derive a kind of perverse superiority from their mastery of the game's ambiguous mechanics. For my part, I don't give a good goddamn if someone has trained themselves to eat shit and like it. The game is not challenging, it's *difficult to play*, and it's taken many years but I'm ready to begin making this distinction."

GETTING DOWN

September 5, 2007 I forgot this strip completely, it's not filed away anywhere in my mind. I like it, though. The technology that underpins a *Metroid* game (which is where all this talk of "spheres" is coming from) is especially baroque, and weirdly custom made for that very rare sort of person who can both turn into a ball *and* has a gun for an arm. If you can only turn into a ball, that ain't gonna cut it. Likewise, if all you have is the gun arm, this is gonna be a real short game.

THE DAWN OF A GLORIOUS NEW AGE

September 7, 2007 There were a series of patches for the PS3 that focused on "compatibility and playability issues for select titles" without saying what titles were benefiting from increased compatibility and playability. What this invariably does is create a kind of mysticism around a particular update, so that people start coming forward claiming it's cured their ills, like true believers at some kind of tent revival.

AN EMBARRASSMENT OF KITTENS

September 10, 2007 Another crazypants thing that people were saying back then (specifically, Sony and its adherents) was that force feedback didn't matter in a controller. It was incredibly silly, especially after having sold us the DualShock before, but whatever. I have to be honest with you, I never went out and bought another Sixaxis when they finally came out with rumble. I have a PS3 and tons of games, sure. But that's a grudge I decided to hold onto, for whatever reason.

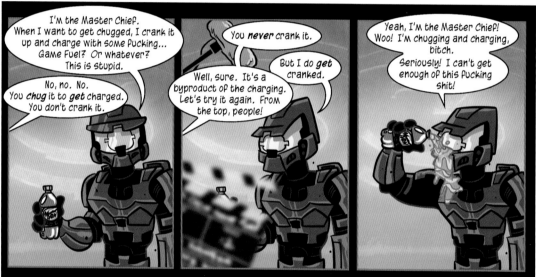

AT LEAST IT'S OVER SOON

September 12, 2007 This was another Launch Title that didn't land quite right, though it had a lot to communicate in the art and story. The game's developer, Ninja Theory, learned a lot about making a narrative game that got plowed into their next game, *Enslaved*. And *Enslaved* frequently glitters with genius. So we're Even Steven, basically. Oh, and they made *Kung Fu Chaos*, which was pretty bad-ass. In terms of Tycho points, they're looking pretty good right now.

ALIEN GENOCIDE IS THIRSTY WORK

September 14, 2007 Ads for "male" sodas are always a problem, but I have to admit that I got hooked on this shit. That's the typical arc: I started drinking it ironically, then I started drinking it for reals. That was until I read the ingredients one day, something I am in the habit of doing, and saw something called "Brominated Vegetable Oil." I didn't know what that was, but it didn't seem especially refreshing. When I think about drinking it now, I feel kind of sick.

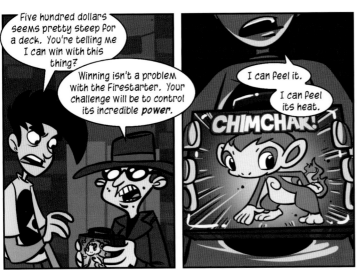

THAT RAVENOUS FIRE

September 17, 2007 Oh, man. Okay. So, like I said, Gabriel (and Kiko, and Amber, and…) got hooked real bad on the Pokeymans. But they got as wrapped up in the CCG too, especially Gabe and Keek, and it turned ugly. Those two warred over slight alterations to decks and authentically nasty combos, with the netdecking you see in panel one plus lots of other surgical purchases. Kiko made a deck that fed off of his opponent's cards, so the only way Gabe would beat it was to make a bad deck.

IN THE LOVE NEST OF HAR'AKKI

September 19, 2007 Further elaborations, from the post: "Where are the bipedal crustaceans in this calculation? The swirling, aroused gasses? The lonely, sentient space station whose hermetic bulkheads hold secret clusters of erotic delights, provided your character has both the skills and equipment? Carpe astrum, you goddamned backwater clowns. There must be an entire universe of thrilling, dangerous, sometimes razor sharp genitalia that slavers beyond the Horsehead Nebula."

THE PROTIP

September 21, 2007 I love to look at *Team Fortress 2* — it's usually one of the first things I pull off Steam to test a new machine. The art, writing, and characterization are essentially the apex. But I *do not* like playing it. I know, I know. It's impossible! But I think I actually hate it. Nothing that happens in a given round has ever made any sense to me. I once described a round of *Team Fortress 2* as "twenty croquet balls banging around in a dryer."

AT THE CORNER OF BAIT AND SWITCH

September 24, 2007 Like I said: I was mad. We cautioned them directly in the post (and in person, whenever I had the luxury of a representative) about saying things that were flatly untrue, which a less diplomatic person might call "hateful lies." This is the kind of weird crap that, aggregated with other missteps and a particularly canny competitor, takes you from a First Place finish to still picking up the pieces years later.

HOW DO YOU CELEBRATE?

September 26, 2007 A storied sub-genre of *Penny Arcade*, comics about Gabriel's birthday constitute a discrete body of work that includes some of my favorite comics. The one that concerns how this day is celebrated "around the world" might be my favorite, as it includes panels devoted to the "Flying Gabriel Rejoice Festival" and "Goerbemisdag." We wrote this strip when I was up in Canada, writing the first chapter of *On The Rain-Slick Precipice Of Darkness*.

BETTER THAN MOWING LAWNS?

September 28, 2007 Essentially, he's operating a "farm," except the sort of thing that he wants done is the sort of thing kids actually want to do all day. When *Diablo 3* turns every player into a Gold Farmer, for themselves and for Blizzard, that will essentially change the world, right? That's cyberpunk — we'd be living in *Neuromancer* or whatever, right? Tell me how it's different. I mean, aside from the fact that you can't project your consciousness digitally. Aside from that.

DARK BUT NOT REALLY

October 1, 2007 That Tycho up in the window is some pretty haunting shit, and could quite possibly haunt a person permanently in a perpetual mega-haunt. Also, this is one of the few times you see the "house" the "characters" live in from the front, simply because we needed to show their lawn. We needed the lawn, so we could have the antelope. You know what I mean? Some of these decisions make themselves. But "Tycho and Gabe" alternately live in a house, an apartment, or a formless void as necessary.

ACTUALLY VERY DARK

October 3, 2007 I had a reputation for stealing people's skulls in *Halo 3*'s multiplayer campaign, which is probably why he would need a young man to seek them out. I didn't even care about the skulls, not really; but if I got a sense that the person I was playing with was into that sort of thing, I usually knew where they were and would take them. Again, you know: I'm not saying that this is a good thing to do, or that I'm a good person. But! Did I help them adjust their priorities a little bit? I like to think so.

THE END OF THE RAINBOW ROAD

October 5, 2007 Firing Mario would probably not be the best plan for Nintendo. No, they fired a woman working for them on contract after discovering her blog, a blog entitled "Inexcusable Behavior." We basically paraphrased her blog for the strip; that's not something we came up with on our own. When I was reading the comic, I was like, "That doesn't really sound like me," and it wasn't. We were borrowing somebody else's weird shit.

MISINFORMATION

October 8, 2007 That is my incredibly beautiful son, Elliot, who will always look like this in my mind, to some extent. That's not something I understood until I had a child of my own: he will hate it, just as I hated it, but you will always be somebody's baby and there's not a whole hell of a lot you can do about it. This was a real answer to a real question he asked. This was also the day he learned the word "pagina," which is not (to my knowledge) a real organ.

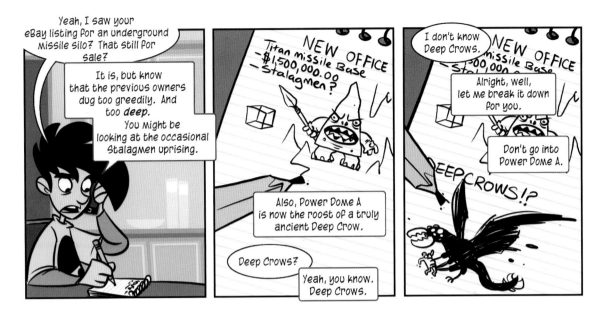

AS SEEN IN MODERN LAIR

October 10, 2007 I still think about this strip constantly, for a lot of reasons. For one, these silos still come up for auction sometimes. There's nothing I would love more than to own something like this. Also, this was the first reference to the *deep crow*, which people seemed to enjoy. It's a bird, but it's also a bug, and its beak goes the wrong way. We've gotten a lot of use out of this thing, which (as you can see here) is really just an odd throwaway line.

THINK OF THE POSSIBILITIES

October 12, 2007 It's worth reminding ourselves that *Portal* — which went on to become a phenomenon slash cultural touchstone — was only one of the games included in the product known as the Orange Box. Valve fans who had followed the company for years already had some of them, but for people like our own Gabriel, receiving *Half Life 2*, the first two Episodes, *Team Fortress 2*, and *Portal* all together represented a spooky, almost overwhelming return on their investment.

INTERDIMENSIONAL VALUES

October 15, 2007 "Denimite" was a material in a song I wrote for Kris Straub, who is a friend of mine now, but wasn't entirely my friend at the time. He's done a lot of cool stuff — *Checkerboard Nightmare*, *Starslip Crisis*, *Blamimations*, the *Kris & Scott Show*, tons of music, a little bit of everything. I really wanted to know a person like that, so I wrote him a song and sent it in an email. The song was about love, I think, as so many of them are.

THIS WEEK'S OBSESSION

October 17, 2007 Like I said, he went in WHOLE HOG on the Pokémania: the switch was flipped, and he went buck-ass wild on every axis. This game wasn't bad at all, either: most of these brand tendrils had something to like about them. The draw here were the beautiful figurines, which you spun inside their special bases to resolve combats. It was similar to a *HeroClix* type base, but *here* the spin itself was the resolution too — there wasn't a dice component at all. Clever, clever stuff.

IT'S SO GODDAMN LATE

October 19, 2007 I imagine it wasn't an especially riveting interview. I do get excited remembering that second panel. Though I'm certain it dates me to say so, this is what young people in my generation were led to believe via movies like *Cloak & Dagger* and *The Last Starfighter*: we were not playing games, or fucking around, not simply frittering away our time like *Mom* said. Oh no. What we were doing was training. And our training would defend an imperiled galaxy! etc.

DARKEST REVELATIONS

October 22, 2007 It's real though, I'm sorry, and now this is something you know forever. Cat butts and the rancid oils they retain in juicy polyps are just a reality for you, now. Again: poorly done on my part, could have been more circumspect re: these asshole cysts. You know? That's on me.

MY DEAREST WISH

October 24, 2007 It seemed impossible, and somehow it still does, but Bioware actually did it: they made a *Star Wars* MMO that takes their *Knights of the Old Republic* setting and lets you play it with your friends. I would have said that was impossible, and may not be a good way to invest your money, but it wasn't my money and therefore it wasn't my choice. At this juncture, I can say that I am glad and even grateful that somebody chose to invest so firmly in what seemed like a fool's errand.

A WRENCH, DESCENDING

October 26, 2007 This shit is grim! *Grim*. But even seeing the characters there in the strip, which are Gabriel's representations of them, I can still hear the *jinga-linga-linga* of those bolts being banged out of a motherfucker. The closest analog I can think of is when my dad let me have five entire dollars at an arcade once. I put it into the change machine, and it made the exact same sound for a comically long period of time. Arcades? What? I'm old; don't forget.

THE REGIMEN

October 29, 2007 This proven system, with its unique dietary requirements and its cold meat, did in fact deliver him success. This was back when he was still playing Ping Pong on the official ladder, before a fateful match where his opponent *dislocated his own shoulder* during the prosecution of his table tennis duties. That was it for Gabriel, and he checked out; the destruction figuratively and literally of an opponent was the apex of his career.

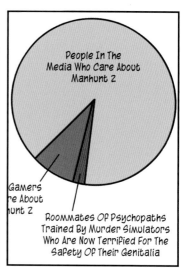

THE DEDICATED GAMES RETAILER EXPERIENCE

October 31, 2007 It's rare that I shop at, well, what it says there in the title of the strip, because usually I can find what I want somewhere else and they won't hassle me for it. They won't tell me they have things when they don't, or tell me to buy things I don't want, or actively warp an industry with their perverse and ancient physicality. Stores like this have completely ceased to be my first choice.

PAINSTAKING MARKET RESEARCH

November 2, 2007 *Manhunt* has always been a "big story" that was never connected to any kind of authentic groundswell among people playing games. I've never played either one, and in my circle of friends there are zero people who played either one outside of the professional reviewers who were literally paid to play it. It was a game that seemed purpose-built to agitate media scolds and to abrade their precious sensibilities. And so, in this way, we may consider it a success. I mean, I sort of get it; I abrade people's precious sensibilities as my job.

THE LITTLEST HASHSHASHIN

November 5, 2007 Most of the portable variants of *Assassin's Creed* have been more or less nonsense. They don't really feel like *Assassin's Creed*, or at any rate they don't seem like what I *think* it is, because for me that means climbing around on ancient churches in a city where I can go anywhere. There's a nice one out for the iPad, though, *Recollections*, which takes the amazing art from the series and cooks up a CCG with it. It's *so* different that it doesn't feel like a partial version of the original concept.

THE SPUR OF THE MOMENT

November 7, 2007 A distillation of the strike, from the post: "The Writers Guild is dealing with the same issues that Musicians have *been* dealing with, that is to say, compensation when the same work takes on a different form in this baffling *digital age*. The way contracts are currently written, there is some magical distinction between content that is broadcast on television, played from a disc, or streamed online. It's hard to imagine there are people who actually claim to believe this kind of mysticism."

LOOTING IS ACTUALLY QUITE CREEPY

November 9, 2007 Looting *is* weird! You're right clicking on a dead creature, and then you get some stuff, but what you're actually doing is going through every pocket, every crease, every fold in a completely systematic way. You're so good at it that you can distill a person into change, saleable merchandise, and useful organs in *one second*. This is something you already knew how to do when you were level one. What in God's name were you doing before?

JOIN THE ALL-STARS

November 12, 2007 It's not a bad job, actually. Obviously, you could do all this stuff yourself, and it's fun. But it reminds me a little of what Patrick Rothfuss calls the "Alar" in his *Kingkiller Chronicle*, splitting your will into different parts. I like the sensation, which is like *mind* juggling different selves. Or, you can give the other controller to a young person or a person who "likes games but not really," and there's enough there to play together.

NITPICKING: MASS EFFECT, PART ONE

November 14, 2007 I loved *Mass Effect*, and I also loved *Mass Effect 2*, but at the time of this writing I don't know whether or not I'll love *Mass Effect 3*. Seems reasonable to guess I will. The Nitpicking parenthetical we use here was something that we'd originally planned to do more of, except that we forgot we'd ever done it. The basic idea was to say, yeah, we like it. Now, over the course of several strips, we'll speak frankly about some of its fucked up shit. We should bring this back.

NITPICKING: MASS EFFECT, PART TWO

November 16, 2007 The first time we saw *Knights of the Old Republic*, we saw it running on the PC where it was originally supposed to be. Then we saw it on the Xbox, and it was good, but not *as* good. These elevators were, I imagine, a concession to the no-hard drive havers and whatever version of the Unreal engine they were using at the time. Intractable, but still a mood killer. How awesome is that gigantic Krogan watch, though? I submit that it is the best!

NITPICKING: MASS EFFECT, PART THREE

November 19, 2007 *Mass Effect 2* felt "more itself" to me, like they had struck a better balance between its shooter ambitions and its RPG heritage than in the first one, so I liked it. That perspective is by no means universal. There were certainly proponents of the first game's greater reliance on fiddly nonsense, which is somehow synonymous with "depth." I like depth, don't get me wrong. But there is a difference between depth and a big blinking sign that merely says "depth, depth, depth" suspended over a few token systems.

FACEBOOKERY

November 21, 2007 Robert told us about this time that Facebook was going to dominate the known universe, and that we'd better get on that shit or we could just forget about becoming Viziers or one of the Low Princes in this new order. Gabriel did so, and I did not, though I suppose "could not" may be more accurate. I can barely keep up with my own goddamned life, and the bottomless need of every person in my immediate circle. Which is bad, because the games on there are starting to get really cool.

FACEBOOK, SUPPLEMENTAL

November 23, 2007 They did create a profile for me eventually, though they had the kindness not to go into a tremendous amount of detail regarding my various enthusiasms. In reality, I imagine that mantasexuals are probably some kind of coveted market, one Facebook almost certainly caters to. They're people with the funds to travel around the globe and screw fish while decked out in entirely custom scuba gear. It's a lucrative demo. Everybody wants a piece.

A DISGUSTING NEW AFFLICTION
NOVEMBER 26, 2007

Let's just get all of our ducks in a row, here.

1. Gabriel doesn't want to go somewhere, so Tycho fashions an excuse for him.

2. Kara knows about the ruse already.

3. Kara thanks Tycho.

Do I have it right? That seems a little high concept, to me. It must have been lunchtime.

THE STORY OF MY LIFE

November 28, 2007 Every few months, Gabriel starts some kind of fight with *some kind of person* and then I have to try to contextualize it because it's my job to… I don't even know what it's my job to do. Write the books, I guess. The main thing to remember is that I am not him. He doesn't go after people with my secret authorization or whatever, I don't want any part of it. I just want to write my little strips and append my little posts and then go home.

THE NEW GAMES JOURNALISM

November 30, 2007 Has this been forgotten entirely, or is it still fresh enough? I guess this book will exist for awhile, being a physical object and everything, so I should probably cover the basics. Jeff Gerstmann, trusted writer for Gamespot, is "said to have been let go" from the aforementioned site as a result of his 6.0 review of the original *Kane & Lynch*. We offered him a job, but he already had one starting up Giant Bomb. Seems like he's doing well over there.

OLD SCHOOL

December 3, 2007 On a visit to his grandparents' house in California before Christmas, the sight of his grandmother's pink DS in the continuum of all her other grandmotherly artifacts made a powerful impression. Then, when he came back, it made an impression on me as well. Just how deep the Wii and the DS got into American culture was incredible to watch. Obviously, it's well outside our normal output. It still needed doing.

INTERESTING CHOICE OF WORDS

December 5, 2007 This was one of the quotes that made Activision CEO Robert Kotick a "name" among game enthusiasts, whose familiarity with him is now such that he is called Bobby. I understand why you would say something like that, but you have to be careful who you say it to, and who they're likely to tell. He presides over the House of Blizzard and *Call of Duty*, though. I imagine he doesn't lose much sleep over it.

IN THE SERVICE OF THE QUEEN

December 7, 2007 In another life, or maybe just later in this one, my cohort and I would like to devote a lot more time to this kind of thing. I think we could get pretty good at it, with enough practice. We'd always meant to do this story as a full book, based on a laser cel we made awhile ago, but we came to terms with the fact that we'd never have time to do it outside of our regular work. So it had to take over for a bit.

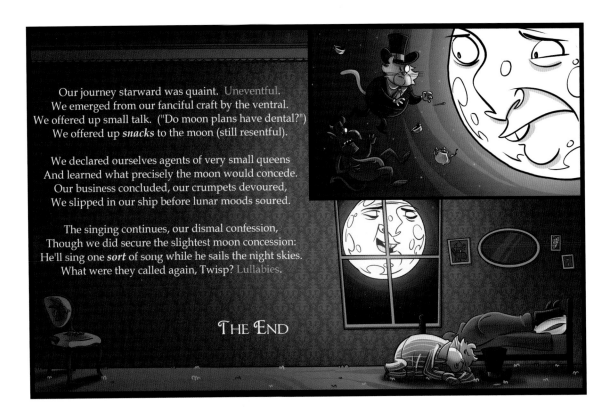

Our journey starward was quaint. Uneventful.
We emerged from our fanciful craft by the ventral.
We offered up small talk. ("Do moon plans have dental?")
We offered up *snacks* to the moon (still resentful).

We declared ourselves agents of very small queens
And learned what precisely the moon would concede.
Our business concluded, our crumpets devoured,
We slipped in our ship before lunar moods soured.

The singing continues, our dismal confession,
Though we did secure the slightest moon concession:
He'll sing one *sort* of song while he sails the night skies.
What were they called again, Twisp? Lullabies.

THE END

IN THE SERVICE OF THE QUEEN, PART TWO

December 10, 2007 That's funny; in my mind, this project is still three pages, and I was shocked to see it end on the second strip. The truth is that there were many forms it could take with six stanzas, three and six pages being the most straightforward options, assuming Gabriel didn't want to get "freaky." It was written to be a book, though, like I said — there's more writing for it somewhere, tucked carefully away in case we ever get a shot at it.

PSEUDONYMS

December 12, 2007 "Handling" the Child's Play Dinner psychologically is quite difficult for me, and I assume for him. Names aren't really my problem; I have systems that help me with that kind of thing. As a generality I feel like I'm faking it whenever I stand in front of people, and maybe everybody feels that way, but I'm almost debilitated by it. And since I have to stand up more and more often as these things have progressed, I spend a greater and greater amount of time feeling strange.

TACHYONS, MY CONSTANT FOE

December 14, 2007 I had never heard of this kind of business arrangement before, and we only heard about it this time because it fell apart: Perpetual ("creators of the *Star Trek* MMO, see above") had secured a company's PR services by cutting them into the profit of the game itself. So when the game was canceled, there was no money. Right? Right. Those must have been some fascinating conversations.

THE GUITAR HERO THING

December 17, 2007 There are many very serious topics upon which we disagree, one of them being whether or not there is a such a creature as a God. But we disagree on smaller things, too, like whether or not Activision should support *Rock Band* controllers in their *Guitar Hero* franchise. If we get into a fight on something, which does happen, we usually try to tie it up in a strip so we can put it to bed. We have a lot to do, and there's not a lot of room in the schedule for this kind of shit.

STRAIGHT TRIPPING

December 19, 2007 I gave them a hard time here, but in truth my normal mode of speaking is largely drawn from late eighties and nineties hip-hop jargon. As a mode of expression that relies on lexicon and persona, there's every reason to believe that I would have been/am currently obsessed with it. Kool Moe Dee's "How Ya Like Me Now" absolutely changed my life. I want to stress the extent to which I'm not joking right now. I'm not. Given the context, though, I would understand why you thought I might be.

THE NEXT-GEN

December 21, 2007 Because he is a villain, you can see from his cookie tray that he is iterating his vile "Dickerdoodles" ritual, whereby he exhorts the readership to make entirely disgusting peepee shaped cookies and make dioramas or pose with them or whatever. This last "batch" was especially nasty, featuring more than one variant of the Nativity reimagined as a blasphemous orgy. If I believed in hell, this would be how you'd get there.

THE DEERLY DEPARTED

December 24, 2007 He really did have one of those novelty, head bobby type lawn deer, and if you can believe it, these wayward youths made off with two of them. He even made a flyer, though don't believe it ever got posted anywhere. That is to say, I hope he didn't post it. But that's not something I can verify and frankly I don't have a lot of faith in the assertion.

LOST!

John Travolta

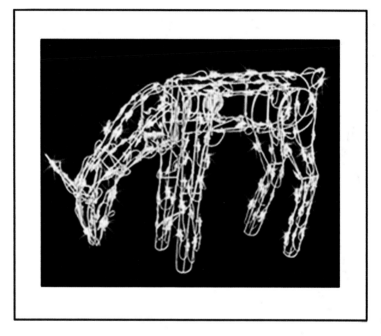

We've lost our deer.
John Travolta is a male, domestic, white lighted, 3 year old deer.

We unfortunately lost him on or around Wednesday the
19th of December from our front yard.

This picture was taken a year ago and since then John Travolta has grown
slightly. He has a bigger tummy and is quite skittish. He may
or may not be lit up.

Please help John Travolta find his home. Our thirteen children
desperately miss their deer.

REWARD!

HAVE A HOLLY, JOLLY XMAS

December 26, 2007 We try not to talk about things like this if we can help it, because as I suggested before, we have shit to do. Where we currently stand is that he believes in God but doesn't go to church or practise anything that resembles religion of any kind, and I'm willing to concede that I don't really *know* with one hundred percent certainty that there absolutely, one hundred percent, is not, could not, and will never be a God. It's good enough for now.

WE'RE RIGHT RETURNS

December 28, 2007 We had already stopped doing the "We're Right" Awards, because we don't really like them anyway and they were mostly guilty filler type material, like the waste paper used to fill out Taco Bell's "Meat." We didn't mind bringing back the form in a joking way to praise *Portal*, though. Gabe was incredibly sick at this time, the kind where you can't move or get out of bed for real as opposed to the one where you'd rather not go to work, and our designer Kiko had to fill in on art duties.

THE UNGIFT, PART ONE

December 31, 2007 Do they still make FigurePrints? I just looked it up, and they do — but they had just started doing them back then, and getting in the queue was hard. Everything else here was true, though, and I really had quit. He had quit in the middle of a bunch of quests, half-way to some set, discouraged but finally free. This threw all that into relief: I'd gotten Kiko one as well, and as the Guild-father, he was able to resurrect the entire operation. I'd started another three year guild cycle, entirely without meaning to.

THE UNGIFT, PART TWO

January 2, 2008 Thanks for reading through another volume of *Penny Arcade*, with the Director's Commentary flag activated. And thank you for the continued opportunity to learn *how* to present ideas in this way, and for the thrice-weekly deadline that has provided my life such purpose and momentum. I appreciate it beyond my capacity to *express* that appreciation.

See you next year.

Gabe Art: The Cover

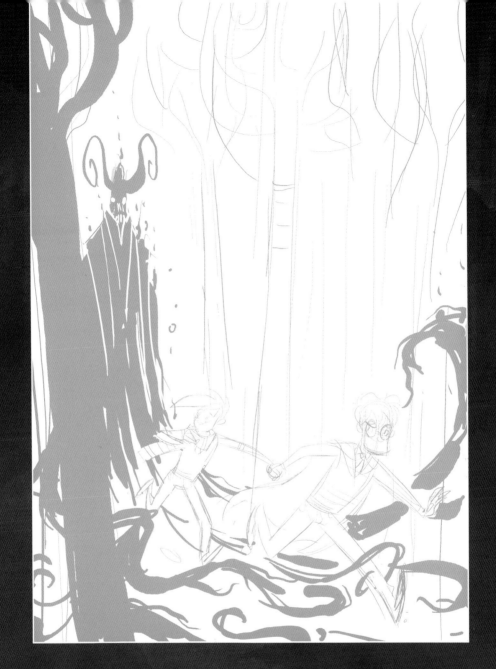

This first image is my initial sketch. I worked for a while in a sketchbook until I hit on a pose I liked and then transferred that into Photoshop. You can see it is extremely rough but it's enough for me to get started.

Here I've completed the inks for Gabe and Tycho. As you can see I decided to make them younger than I had originally sketched them. At first I sort of saw them as teenagers but as I started working on the cover I felt like it might be more fun if they were little kids.

I've added the monster now. I want him to be mostly made up of shadow so I don't do much more than his head. I figure I'll handle the rest when I start doing the colors.

I'm coloring the kids separate from the monster so that I can arrange them as needed in the final composition. I gave Tycho a bit of a Harry Potter vibe and tried to make Gabe a little Jim Darkmagic.

I really liked this monster. Again, I colored him on his own so that I could move him around if need be. I achieve all my glow effects by using the airbrush tool on a layer above my inks. Then I set that layer to "screen" in the layer options and you can see the result in the glow inside his eyes.

I start painting the background using basic fall colors. I use a lot of different brushes here, as well as adjusting the opacity of various layers, to get the painterly look I am after.

I wanted to set it at night, so I gave the entire image a purple tint. Next, I started dropping in my various texture layers. These are usually set to the "overlay" option in Photoshop and their opacity is brought way down. This part takes a lot of fiddling until I get it looking just like I want it.

And then I was finished.

OTHER BOOKS FROM ONI PRESS...

SCOTT PILGRIM:
PRECIOUS LITTLE BOX SET
Bryan Lee O'Malley
digest, b&w, includes poster
ISBN 978-1-934964-57-6

SCOTT PILGRIM: SPECIAL EDITION
VOLUME1, HARD COVER
Bryan Lee O'Malley
184 pages, hardcover, color
ISBN 978-1-62010-000-4

THE SIXTH GUN, VOLUME 1:
COLD DEAD FINGERS
Cullen Bunn, Brian Hurtt, Bill Crabtree
176 pages, trade paperback, color
ISBN 978-1-934964-60-6

SIDESCROLLERS
Matthew Loux
216 pages, digest, b&w
ISBN 978-1-932664-50-8

BLACK METAL, VOLUME 1:
THE GRIM RETURN
Rick Spears & Chuck BB
160 pages, digest, b&w
ISBN 978-1-932664-72-0

SHARKNIFE, VOLUME 1:
STAGE FIRST
Corey Lewis
168 pages, digest, b&w
ISBN 978-1-934964-64-4

For more information on these and other fine Oni Press comic books and graphic novels visit onipress.com. To find a comic specialty store in your area visit comicshops.us.

Oni Press logo and icon ™ & © 2012 Oni Press, Inc. Oni Press logo and icon artwork created by Keith A. Wood.